The Orphan Calf
and the Magical Cheetah

Cheetah poems, essays and illustrations by the Namibian people

Compiled by Stephen DeVincent, DVM

New Namibia Books

New Namibia Books
P.O. Box 21601
Windhoek
Namibia

Cheetah Conservation Fund
P.O. Box 247
Windhoek
Namibia

First published in 1996
Copyright: Artwork © Shell Art Competition,1994.
Copyright: Text © Cheetah Conservation Fund (CCF) 1996.

Much of the factual information has come from the CCF's Teacher's Resource Guide, *Cheetahs: A Predator's Role in the Ecosystem*.

Design: John T. O'Connor

Production and Typography: Katherine L. Pestana

Manuscript Editor: Catherine E. Olofson

Color Separations: Typographic House

Printed in Namibia by Capital Press

ISBN: 99916-31- 54-2

To Gizzy
who allowed us to share her cheetah world and from
whom we developed a greater appreciation for her and her brethren.

She is missed by all of us who were fortunate enough
to look into her beautiful golden eyes,
observe her delicate walk and
listen to her purrs of affection.

With love and a commitment
to improve the fate of her feline species.

Foreword

The inspiration to produce *The Orphan Calf and the Magical Cheetah* came from the enthusiastic response by Namibia's youth to two competitions that took place in 1994, initiated by Kristin Sarri of the Cheetah Conservation Fund (CCF). The Shell Art Competition was organized jointly by the Desert Ecological Research Unit of Namibia, Arts Directorate of the Ministry of Education and Culture, National Art Gallery and Shell Namibia Ltd. The Cheetah Writing Competition was sponsored and organized by the Cheetah Conservation Fund.

The aim of the art competition was to give young Namibians the opportunity to express their appreciation of the natural environment through painting and drawing. The theme "Predators" was chosen to encourage participants to think about the important role that Namibia's lions, cheetahs, leopards, jackals, wild cats and birds of prey play in the ecological balance of our natural world. The competition was open to all pupils at primary and secondary schools in Namibia.

The theme of the writing competition was more specific. It concerned the cheetah and its race for survival, seen in the context of Namibia's being home to the world's largest population of free-ranging cheetah, approximately 2 500 of an estimated global population of 12 500. As the Cheetah Capital of the world, Namibia holds the key to this unique animal's continued existence. Over 800 entries were received for the writing competition, which was open to primary and secondary school pupils, as well as to older students and adults.

By expressing in poems, essays and short stories their personal view of the cheetah's habits, characteristics, appearance and role in the ecosystem, the participants not only have broadened their own perspectives regarding the dilemma of this beautiful and endangered animal but also, in a wider sense, have committed themselves to promote its future survival. Children will pass the message on to their parents, many of whom are the farmers on whose land Namibia's remaining cheetahs range. Through the dedicated work of the CCF and other individuals, the perception that cheetahs are nothing more than a threat to livestock is gradually giving way to a recognition of the cheetah's right to exist as a precious natural asset deserving of its own particular niche in the environment. Publications such as this can only serve to enhance this process.

As one of the judges of the writing competition, I was struck by the scope of writing talent that emerged. The content of the entries ranged from personal appreciations of the cheetah's beauty and its plight to more concrete, factual descriptions of this intriguing animal. The ideal would be to publish all the entries, but sadly this is not possible. The artwork, poems, essays and short stories chosen for this volume include tributes to the cheetah's speed and hunting prowess; fanciful tales of how the cheetah got its spots; and more harshly realistic depictions of cheetahs falling prey to poachers or cubs being orphaned because their mother has been shot or caught in a trap. I trust that these works will serve to both inform and uplift the reader.

Amy Schoeman

Overview of the Cheetah in Namibia

Namibia has the largest remaining population of free-ranging cheetahs in the world (approximately 2 500 animals). It also supplies most of the imports of wild cheetahs to the world's zoos, whose populations are not self-sustaining.

Namibia is the first country in the world to include sustainable utilization of wildlife and protection of its environment in its constitution, intending to ensure the availability of a large prey base that can sustain a healthy population of cheetah. However, cheetah populations in Namibia continue to decline due to loss of habitat, reduction in the numbers of prey and conflict with livestock farming. Complicating the situation is the cheetah's lack of genetic diversity, making the species more susceptible to ecological and environmental changes.

Ninety percent of the cheetah population of Namibia lives outside of protected game reserves. Principally, in Namibia, cheetahs are found on commercial livestock farmland (ranches) that raise cattle, sheep and goats and have free-ranging populations of wildlife. Most Namibian farmers have a great disdain for cheetah, as they prey on their livestock. Cheetahs are known to kill small-stock (sheep and goats) and calves up to six months of age. Farmers have often killed cheetahs, whenever possible, whether there is loss of their livestock or not. The cheetah is blamed for many more losses of livestock and game than actually occur.

The 1975 Nature Conservation Ordinance classifies the cheetah as a protected animal in Namibia. However, the same ordinance further stipulates that a person may shoot a cheetah in order to protect his or her own life or property. The problem for Namibian cheetahs is that most farmers practice preventive management, eliminating cheetahs randomly either by shooting them or catching them in live traps. Because of this ongoing conflict with the farmer, the cheetah population in Namibia has been drastically reduced.

Photograph of Gizzy by Karen Terio

In order better to assess the situation of the cheetah in Namibia today, an in-depth survey with commercial farmers has been underway since 1991 in districts of the country where cheetahs still exist. The purpose of the survey is to develop baseline data identifying general statistics, cheetah distribution patterns, overall land conditions and prey availability. The survey also includes farmers' interactions with cheetah and other wildlife, numbers of livestock and current livestock and game management practices.

Some Namibian farmers have found workable solutions to their confrontation with the cheetah. Donkeys have been used to protect a farm in Otjiwarongo since 1986. The donkeys are aggressive towards cheetahs and chase them away. Other positive approaches include locating calving camps closer to a homestead, more closely monitoring heifer herds (they are less protective mothers and have more problematic births) and raising a more aggressive breed of cattle such as Brahman. Farms with more wildlife have been found to have fewer problems with predation as there is more natural prey for the predators. Success has also been achieved on a small number of farms through the proper installment and management of electric fence systems.

The loss of small-stock has been effectively reduced through the use of herders and special dogs. The Anatolian Shepherd, a large breed guarding dog originally from Turkey, has been successful in limiting small-stock losses on a growing number of farms throughout cheetah territory.

In Namibia, free-ranging cheetahs, which have adapted to the farmlands, move through very large ranges of over 1 500 square kilometers. In these ranges they exhibit behaviors unlike cheetahs in other parts of Africa. One unique behavior is the strong drive of cheetahs to go to "playtrees" (tall trees with sloping trunks), and observe their surroundings from the horizontal limbs. Not all farms in Namibia have playtrees, and cheetahs move quickly through these farms on their way to the next playtree.

Cheetahs are often caught at playtrees in live traps. The drive of the cheetah to reach a playtree is so strong that it will readily use the trap as a passageway and walk in, triggering the metal doors. Once caught, some of the cheetah are exported to zoos, while others are shot and killed. The majority of this trapping is indiscriminate, not necessarily involving problem cheetahs. This type of elimination often increases the problem for the farmers as territories are opened and other cheetahs move into the area trying to find a territory.

The fate of Namibia's wildlife, including the cheetah, is in the hands of Namibia's farmers. Therefore, strategies to save populations of wildlife for the future must be integrated with livestock management. Development of these strategies is dependent on the willingness of the local communities, and their full understanding of all aspects of the ecosystem. Therefore, research on cheetahs in Namibia needs to be focused on providing specific information so that wise management choices can be made.

For cheetah to survive in Namibia, they must have abundant habitat, a solid prey base and a holistic management approach on the farmlands on which they roam. Namibia, with its varied ecosystems and commitment to the environment, poses the greatest hope worldwide for the future of the cheetah.

Laurie Marker-Kraus
Daniel Kraus
Co-Directors, Cheetah Conservation Fund

The Call of Namibia

When you've acquired a taste for dust,
The scent of our first rain,
You're hooked for life on Namibia,
And you'll not be right again
Till you can watch the setting moon
And hear the cheetah's call
And know that they're around you,
Waiting in the dark.

When you long to see the elephants
Or hear the coucal's song,
When the moonrise sets your blood on fire,
You've been away too long.
It's time to cut the traces loose
And let your heart go free
Beyond that far horizon,
Where your spirit yearns to be.

Namibia is waiting – come!
Since you've touched open sky
And learned to love the rustling grass,
The wild fish eagle's cry,
You'll always hunger for the bush,
For the cheetah's breath,
To camp at last beneath the stars
And to be at peace once more.

E.E. Botha

There are an estimated 7 000 commercial farms in
Namibia, encompassing about 49 percent of the country.
Approximately 90 percent of the cheetahs in Namibia are
found in the North Central Commercial Livestock
Farmlands owned by about 1 000 farmers.

Anna Shiluwa, Age 16

Marletta de Villiers, Age 12

Cheetah

The well-known
The fastest
The beautiful
Unbeatable

Soft movements
Soft tones
Our cheetah
Our pride

Simon Brinkman, Grade 10

Cheetah

Sad sprinter
unique lonely hunter
predator that is endangered
misunderstood

Benjamin Tshabalala, Grade 7

The indigenous peoples of southern Africa considered the cheetah part of their natural environment. The San Bushmen, for example, did not normally hunt the animal for meat but are said to have eaten its flesh only in times of extreme need. They used these cheetah skins as cloaks and the bones of the feet as spiritual symbols believing that they would give them fleet-footedness.

Cheetahs and leopards were known as Izolo ze Nkosi (Royal Game) amongst the Zulu. These animals were often used to test the courage of men who were about to be promoted to the position of battle leader. This test consisted simply of sending the men out to bring back a live cat for the chief to look at; then the men would take it back where they had found it and release it.

Once found throughout Asia and Africa, the species is now scattered only in Iran and sub-Saharan Africa. In Namibia, home ranges – areas where cheetahs live and roam – can be as large as 1 500 square kilometres for males and 1 200 - 1 500 square kilometres for females. Individual cheetahs can move 13 to 26 kilometres per day.

Die Jagluiperd

In die maanlig sien ek 'n figuur
'n mooie dier wat in die verte tuur
Jy, geel en kolletjieskat,
Jou ongelukkigheid maak my sat.

Liewe katjie wat is jy?
'n wonderlike dier,
gebou met krag en spier.

Met traanmerke oor jou gelaat,
Is jy 'n un'eke gesig.

O, ek wil jou so graag sien,
maar ek kan nie.
Want vandag lewe jy,
maar môre is jy dood.

Wat gaan van jou word?

The Cheetah

I see a figure in the moonlight,
A beautiful animal gazing into the distance.
You, yellow-spotted cat,
Your unhappiness moves me deeply.

Dear little cat, what are you?
A wonderful animal,
built with power and muscle.

With tearmarks on your face,
you are a unique sight.

Oh, I would so love to see you,
but I can't.
Because today you are alive,
but tomorrow you will be dead.

What will become of you?

Thamara Visser, Grade 9
Original in Afrikaans

Jessica Ulrich, Age 13

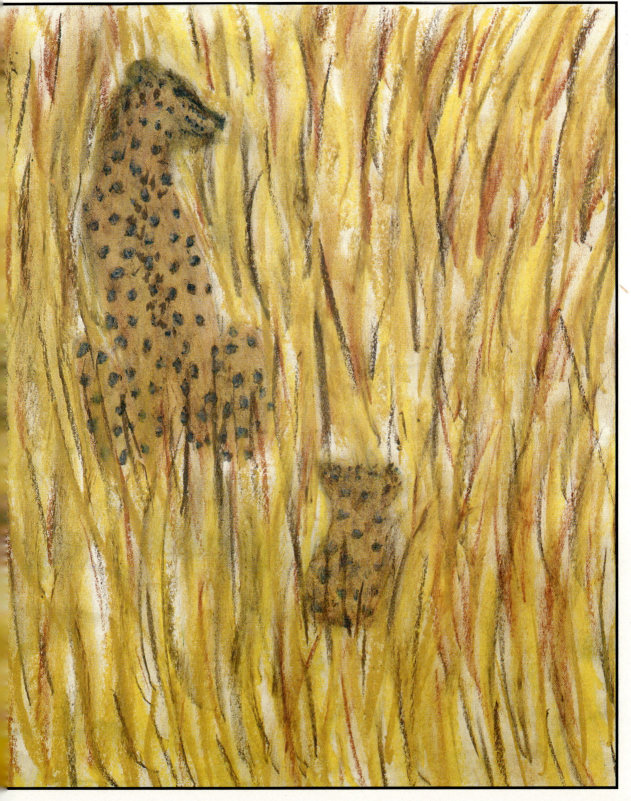

Acinonyx Jubatus

A lone in a world of selfishness, the
C heetah, vulnerable in its nature,
I ntends to live in peace and freedom.
N early extinct, for which we are to blame,
O ften mistaken for a leopard, a
N on-aggressive animal – the cheetah.
Y ears of hardship and suffering and now
X tinction is threatening our unique cat.

J ailed in this decaying world,
U ndeniably the human's fault,
B egging to live in peace and freedom,
A erodynamic and unique,
T he cheetah's adapted features,
U nwanted among other predators,
S ociable among his kind – the cheetah.

J ust a few people prepared to fight extinction,
U nmercifully left to its fate by the rest of the world.
B eyond peace and freedom, the cheetah lives in an
A ggressive and violent world,
T ortured by the "wisest" creatures on earth.
U nconcern of most of us finally causes the failure of
S urvival of our unique cat – the cheetah.

Nadine Bingel, Grade 11

The cheetah, Acinonyx jubatus, *is the sole member of its genus. After the mass extinction during the Pleistocene epoch some 10 000 years ago, all but one species of Africa, Asia, Europe and North America* jubatus, *became extinct.*

kurt
cheetah
round kidne
tears mus
soft
bristly

Kurt Normann, Grade 1

1

es

Estelle Rautenbach, Age 11

A Tear

From a distance there is a tear,
Receiving one, but stalking all.
The dark eye watches you from
Within the tall grasses.
Comes closer,
The muscles become tense,
Suddenly there is dust of speed,
A strong body curved with strength
Gets his one.
As he lies with pride,
You will notice
The tear is a cry
For Survival.

Cindy Du Toit, Grade 9

Even though game reserves protect many species, cheetahs are not doing well in reserves mainly due to competition from more aggressive predators such as lions, leopards and hyenas.

Cheetahs have an important place in the ecosystem. They are predators and therefore are on top of the food chain. Cheetah help eliminate the sick, old and injured animals from the wild, leaving the healthy animals to survive and breed.

The cheetah kills its own prey and does not feed on animals killed by other predators. However, it rarely eats all of the animal, and therefore leaves food for other animals to eat.

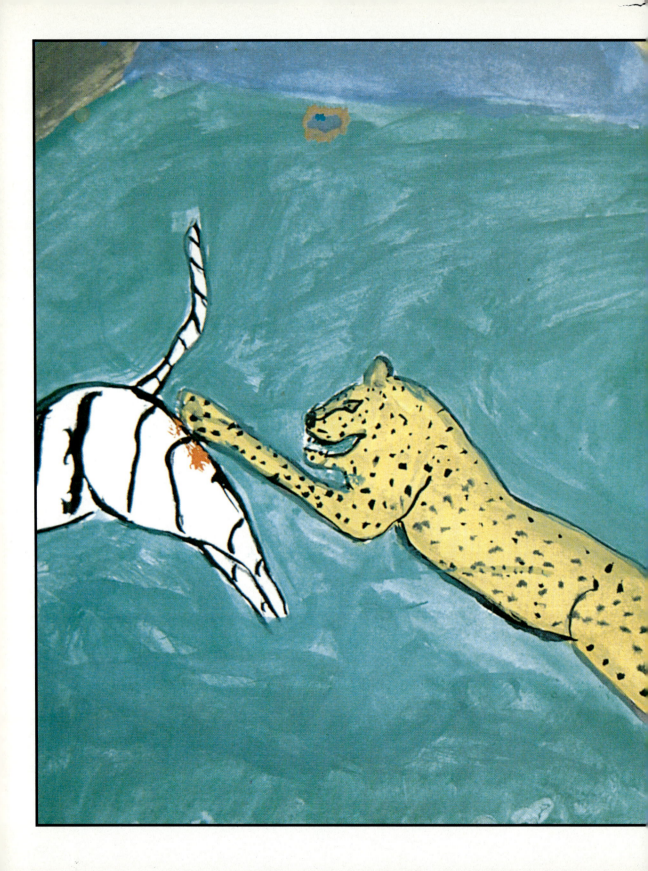

Love Song to a Cheetah

thighs sprung, spine flexed,
your large heart gulps the air
in a stream of cheetah speed.
you claw through cumulus dust
to shift the earth with traction pads.

if I were a shaman from psychic times
I'd embrace your creature shape.

I'd live a long captivity
stalking for mogul and sultan,
funnelling the hunt
in a breeze-streak,
a fine head slipping wind,
eye-line locked on a pulse,
running the buck to ground.

as continents shifted
their great-bulk gravity,
I'd trace your spoor,
nails splayed on a four-paw print,
bridging land to Africa.

here I watch you mark thorn groves
thick with playing trees,
flop a rag-doll body in a fork,
then fling your dark-spot desert yellow
scented through the endless veld.

in a time of fences and predators,
sperm whithers in your feline cave
that rarely echoes the chirp of cubs.

my shy one, elusive as a Namib cloud,
where will you run, my love?
how will you leap to life in the long grass?

Dorian Haarhoff, Adult

Alex Keibel, Age 15

Otjitotongwe

Tjiku tjomuriro otjinawanga!
Ohakahana otje orutjeno rwombura!
Mohakahana wa zepa nu wa ri
Okaravarava aayo wa ţondjara!
Ovengi ve ku isana Tjiwakombanda.

Ozombaze mehi ozondarazu
Kohambana nu konyenyene
Omutima owokazera
Oumumandu omu u ri
Oove ouwe waNamibia.

Oowee, musya wongwe!
Oowee, tjitotongwe nomuinyo waNamibia!

Cheetah

Rocket with poison!
Fast like the lightning of the rain!
Hastily you kill and eat.
Slender as if you starve of hunger,
Many call you beautiful,
Tjiwakombanda.

Feet on the soil are soft,
You never carry on and boast.
The heart belongs to a bird.
Therein is cowardice.
You are the beauty of Namibia.

Oh, child of the tiger's sister!
cheetah and the life of Namibia!

Gabriël Ngungaa Hangara, Grade 11
Original in OtjiHerero

Can the Cheetah Survive?

N amibia is now the capital
A mong the world countries
M ore cheetahs are found here
I t is internationally recognized
B ut this is not enough
I nforming people is the solution
A ction must be taken

C an the cheetah survive?
H ere stands the question
E asy for almost anyone
E ducated or uneducated
T ry to answer it positively
A nimals need security
H ow can we defend them

C ome on fellow Namibians
A nd join the nature conservationists
P articipate fully in this issue
I nform others around you
T hat cheetah has a unique role
A n animal made for speed
L and's only fastest animal

Naminga AA Pellix

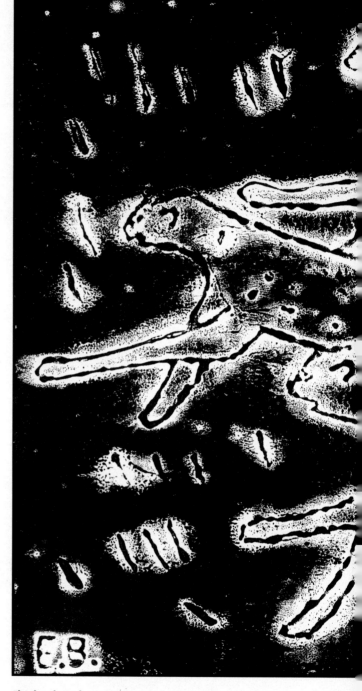

Eberhardt Buchmann, Age 14

Cheetahs are non-aggressive and do not pose a threat to humans.

In Namibia, cheetahs have been found in a variety of habitats, including grasslands, dense vegetation and mountainous terrain.

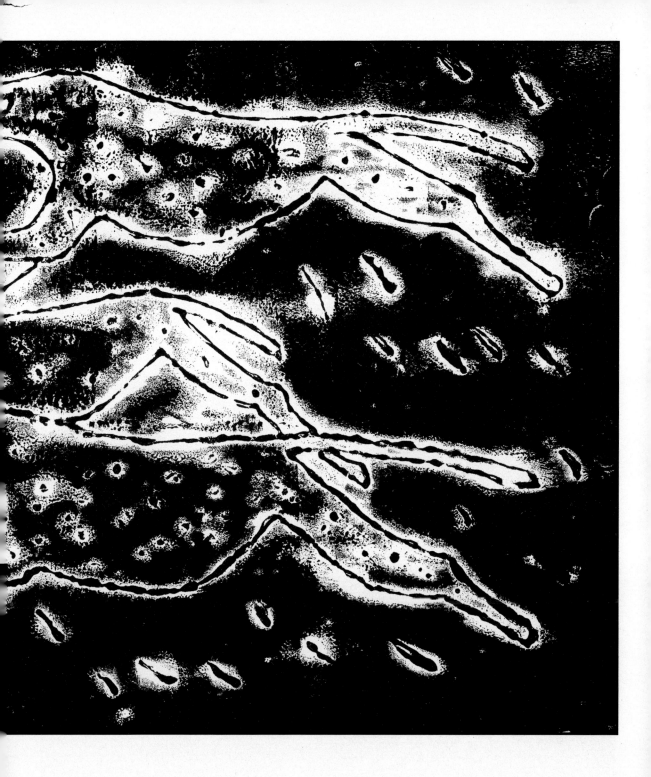

The Cheetah

A cheetah, what is a cheetah? Is it a car, a boat?
Will an African ever ask this question?

Once upon a time, not so long ago, there lived an animal in Africa called the
cheetah. It was a big spotted, light brown cat. It was very fast on the plain,
chasing after its prey. The fastest animal in the world on its feet. The pride of
Africa, beautiful and graceful as it moved through the grass and over the stones.

Each one had its own territory, protected with dignity. It brought up its young
and made them become the hunters of Africa.
But then...

Man began to move around with their own domestic animals, from place to place,
wherever there was green grass. The wild animals moved away or were killed
by man.

The cheetah now had to move. But wait! The man had its animals, easy prey, we
have to eat! That is what many cheetahs did and man killed them trying to
"protect" his animals.

The number of cheetah dwindled and that of man increased. A lot of places for
man to live, not enough room for cheetah to move.
What does this mean? The cheetah will die out!
We will never see the cheetah again.

Is this what we want to hear or read someday?
"No," but it will happen, and the cheetah will only be seen in pictures, and
maybe in some zoos where they will have to sit in a cage and not feel the freedom
to run and hunt.

This won't happen if we all try to help through some organization to protect the
cheetah. Then only will our children know and see the cheetah in the wild.

Act now, and tell your friends and family to help those who are trying to save and
protect the cheetah from the rest of us who don't care.

Willem Du Toit, Age 18

*Cheetahs have existed on earth for about four million years – the longest of any of the large cats
that are alive today. About 20 000 years ago, cheetahs were common throughout Africa, Asia,
Europe and North America. Approximately 10 000 years ago, at the end of the ice age, the
world's environment underwent drastic changes in climate. Over a few thousand years, 75
percent of the mammal species in America, Europe and Asia vanished. When the mammals
began to die, so did all of the cheetahs in North America and Europe, and most of those in Asia
and Africa.*

Kanhi Olivia Fudeni

Help

Is there anyone out there who cares?

Looking through metal bars at the world I have no part in, the outside world.
A world which now has fallen apart for me.

I am one of the last of my kind and have no place to go. My place with wide open
spaces, and golden fields, where I am free, has all been destroyed by man and
his evil ways.

The cage I am standing in is cold and damp.
I was put here for a reason. The reason to regain that which man has destroyed
and that is the cheetah species. My world does not exist, so
man will now decide where I will go and how to replace me.

Will there be a life for me tomorrow?
Time is running out. I need all the support and strength I can get to survive.

Man is the cause. He must reach out to me in
any way instead of hunting me down.

If you care, help fight, before it is too late!

Kathryn McLean, Grade 11

The Cheetah's Heritage

Cheetahs have been around for ages.
They don't deserve to be locked in cages.
They don't deserve to be shot and skinned.
Why do people do that?
Have the cheetahs sinned?
We have to do the best we can
To save the cheetahs and their land.
The cheetahs do deserve
To be loved and preserved.

Aneesha Mayman, Grade 7

*Cheetahs prefer wild game to livestock, but they are opportunistic and if they are unable to find
or catch wild game, they may resort to taking livestock if the animals are unprotected or
vulnerable. Domestic animals are easier prey than wild animals because they are much slower
and less able to escape the attack of a predator. Most predators do not seek our domestic
livestock, but prefer wild prey as it stimulates their natural predatory instincts.*

Elsabe Jooste, Grade 9

Shinga – The Cheetah

Shinga, whose name means "Cheetah," was born in the northeast, in Owamboland. He has one brother and one sister. The three cubs are two years old. Shinga has a small round head, a thin waist and a big chest. His tail is long and thick, which will help him to turn quickly when he is chasing after his prey. His legs are long and he can run very fast over a short distance.

Shinga's face always looks as if he has been crying. He has two black lines which run from his eyes to the corners of his mouth. But Shinga is not a sad cheetah, because he lives freely on a farm in Namibia. His coat is pale brown and spotted all over. The spots are round and black. This makes it easier for him to hide in the bush. He is not like other cats because he cannot pull in his claws.

But the cubs do have enemies...
Shinga and the other cubs have the lion and man as their enemies, so the people of Namibia must help to save them.

Ryan Thompson, Grade 4

A Cheetah in Namibia

I am a cheetah and I am very fond of playing. I specially like to play in my playtree. I also like to lie on a rock in the mountains and to watch everybody.

From my playtree I can see where the hares make their burrows and then I can make my plans how to catch them.

I am a pretty tan colour with small black spots on my coat. I like to eat fresh meat, especially that of warthogs, hares, birds and steenbock.

I play an important role to ensure a healthy ecosystem.

I do hope everybody in this beautiful country will realise it and save me from an unnatural death. Please help me survive in Namibia.

Saima Ashipala

The average weight of an adult cheetah is 34-54 kilograms. Its body length ranges from 112-135 centimetres. Its length from head to tail is 66-84 centimetres, and its shoulder height is 73+ centimetres. The male is slightly larger than the female.

Cheetahs make chirping sounds, and hiss or spit when they are angered or threatened. They purr very loudly when they are content.

Maneke Bays, Age 10

Save the Cheetah

S uperb animal
A nd great camouflage in the wild
V ery good sense of hearing
E xtraordinarily small for predator

T he speed of it is faster than most cars
H as very good eyesight
E ats meat that it has killed by itself

C unning but shy
H as little strength
E ndurance is little after the chase
E specially if the prey is fast
T ail used as a rudder
A bility to control speed
H ave got to save it!

Thurein Paing, Erik Clacey and Vusi Moyo, Grade 7

The cheetah's long and muscular tail acts as a stabilizer or rudder. The tail helps the cheetah keep its balance when it makes quick turns, by going side-to-side during a high-speed chase.

Will the Cheetah Survive?

When Africa was young and untamed,
it was said that the mighty Lion ruled.
He was the one who had all the power.
He decided on life and death, he was the one that ruled.

At his side was his loving wife, the Cheetah.
Being the fastest animal on four feet,
she covered the vast African plains from North to South, from East to West.
With her wisdom and his strength,
they became an international symbol.
A symbol of Africa, a symbol of our ancestors,
a symbol of unity and love, a symbol known in every mind.

Today, the symbol of our ancestors,
the symbol of hope has disappeared through our hands.
With the power in our hands, we became the rulers of Africa!

The cry of humans, thousands of humans, fill the African plains today.
We have become victors over the wild, we have won the lion.
We have destroyed the once mighty ruler of Africa!

But humans are still inconsiderate,
we don't recognize our mistakes.
Never again can we bring back what we have destroyed.
Only we can decide whether the Cheetah will survive or not,
whether it will be free again, able to go where it wants to,
whether our humanity will show mercy to what God has created.

Again and again one question comes to mind.
Will the Cheetah survive?

Only we can decide the answer to that question.
The power of love and the need for freedom can cause the
Cheetah to live forever, free!

Andries Alberts, Age 16

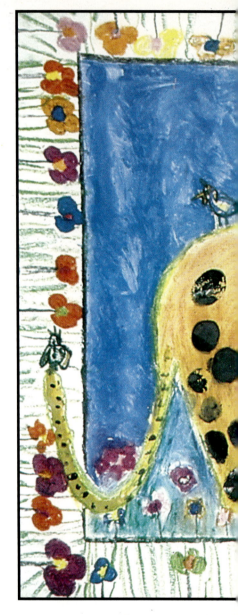

Artist Unknown

*The number of cheetahs has decreased from 100 000 at
the turn of the century to approximately 12 500 today.*

Reflections

A soft cushion at my neck, a cup of strong hot coffee, what more could I want? Why do I bother to read through pages and pages of bad news? Why do I hold this particular book in my hand – and not one of those romantic love stories?

I am just about to put the heavy "Book of Endangered Species" away when I turn the pages and a look strikes me with a full blow. As I turn back the pages to find the accusing eyes, I find myself looking into the most alive photo of a cheetah I have *ever* seen.

Captured by the eyes, I stare back into the glare, trying to escape the hypnosis. Forgotten is the love story, forgotten is all the comfort I had just a few minutes ago. All that matters at this moment are these expressive eyes and the story they have to tell.

Just the head of a cheetah appears in the photogragh, with small ears and a light fur color with black spots here and there. In the shining dark of the retinas there seems to be a flash, a spark of strength and determination. There is no cruelty, coldness or beastliness in the eyes, as one would expect in a big, wild cat. This is no lion or leopard, eager to fight and dominate.

The eyes convey a certain shyness. They give it confidence in its speed and its agility. It will always outrun all the other animals on the flat plains; it will always be able to flee if danger comes. The coffee next to me cools off while images flow over me. The slim hunter speeding graciously over the savannas...

After looking at the picture now more curiously than hypnotized, I'm trying to find out what made me look twice in the first place. It was not the striking colors or the shy but determined look in the eyes... it was the sadness the picture conveyed. The fact that it was in *this* book, among those of the depressingly growing list of endangered animal species.

And on the whole, the cheetah seems to be a symbol of the sealed fate of *all* the animals on Earth. The dark tearmarks symbolize the tears nature cries, its sobs. Why don't we hear them? Why are we so deaf to the sounds, the instincts, the calls of nature, while they should be most important and natural to us?

We hear only money calling, in a deeper captivating voice. The soothing song of wealth lulls us into a dream based on the need for comfort and status of modern man. In a monotone but convincing tone technology urges us to make new discoveries. We hear all that, but we have lost the gift to listen to nature. And so nature cries, and those of the cheetah stay unheard.

Birgit Einbeck, Grade 12

Amina Baird, Age 7

Will the Cheetah Survive?

The cheetah is the fastest land animal but is now travelling faster than ever to extinction. In pre-colonial times the cheetah could be found all over India and the Middle East. It lived everywhere in Africa, except for the Namib and parts of the Sahara desert and in the dense equatorial rain forest.

Since then, many cheetahs have been trapped alive to be sold, shot or poisoned because they supposedly destroy livestock or have simply died due to destruction of their habitat and prey. Now they are limited to much smaller numbers in east and southern Africa and a few scattered groups in the Middle East and West Africa.

Namibia is the cheetah's last stronghold, with a population of about 3 000, but even these are under threat from human beings, and their numbers are reduced every week. There have been efforts by many concerned people to save the cheetah from extinction and limit human damage to these animals. But has enough been done or is it too little, too late?

Threats To Cheetah Survival

In the national parks of Namibia, such as Etosha, cheetahs are protected. The majority, however, are found outside these areas. Under current laws, a farmer is allowed to kill or capture an animal that depletes his stock. Although cheetahs do not usually do this, it is impossible to prove in individual cases, and many farmers do it in the knowledge that they can earn a lot of money from either the sale of the skins or of the live animal.

Almost all cheetahs in zoos around the world come from Namibia. However, the cheetah does not breed well (and usually does not breed at all) in captivity. Therefore, when a cheetah dies, the zoo will have to catch another wild one to replace it. Often cheetahs (as well as other animals) are badly treated in transport to their new homes. Keeping cheetahs in captivity could one day be a solution to the problem but at the moment is only worsening it.

In the country's national parks, poaching is becoming a major problem. In other African countries it has reached crisis proportions. This has not yet happened here, but, as there is a high demand for cheetah skin, clothes, and other products, poaching will probably increase unless urgent measures are taken against it.

Saving The Cheetah

This situation is, however, not without hope. A lot is being done to secure the future of the world's fastest land animal. First, much progress has been made in

Artist Unknown

eliminating poaching from Namibian national parks, due to cooperation between the police and the communities living in or around the national parks.

Education about the danger the cheetah is in has been carried out extensively by the Cheetah Conservation Fund (CCF) and the Ministry of Nature Conservation, and this should help to make people aware that cheetah conservation is undoubtedly necessary.

More research is being conducted into breeding cheetahs in captivity. If cheetahs can be bred successfully in captivity, it will eliminate the need to catch wild ones, and eventually those cheetahs born in captivity may be brought back into the wild.

A project was started recently to use specially trained dogs to guard livestock, the idea is that the dogs would scare predators away from the livestock, only killing them if they actually attacked the sheep and goats. This is fairer than shooting them on sight. It is hoped that livestock guard dogs will one day be used all over the country.

Protection of natural resources (including animals) is guaranteed in the Namibian Constitution. The survival of cheetahs in Namibia is one of the many issues we have to deal with to make the Constitution work in practice.

Hugh Ellis, Grade 8

Cheetahs are considered "top predators" – relatively large animals that are carnivores, strictly meat eaters, and usually are not preyed upon by other animals. Because cheetahs need a lot of space in which to find food and mates and to raise their young, they, like other predators, are having trouble surviving on land converted for human use. With the development of commercial farms in Namibia, most of the larger predators have been killed or have sought other territory. Today cheetah and leopard are the primary carnivores found on commercial livestock farmlands in Namibia.

Guarding Dog

There once was a herd of cows. They were having a lot of trouble. Every time a cow gave birth to a calf, a cheetah would come to the farm and attack the newborn calf. One day the farmer decided to buy a dog to see if it would protect his cows. A few months after the dog had been with the cows, a cheetah came. The dog started barking loudly. As soon as the cheetah heard the dog's bark, he turned around and ran away. The farmer learned that he could save his livestock from the cheetahs and also save the cheetah.

Mackenzie Miles, Grade 4

Juvenile cheetahs rely on their mothers to teach them how to hunt and capture wild game. If their mother is indiscriminately killed by a farmer, the young cheetahs may not be able to hunt wild prey and could turn to livestock as a food source, thus becoming problem animals.

The cheetah is the only cat that has semi-retractable claws, as they cannot fully retract them. A cheetah's claws work like the cleats on a track shoe. They dig into the ground as the cheetah pushes off, helping the animal build up speed fast. Like other cats, however, cheetahs run on their toes. This allows them to make sudden turns without losing their balance.

Aniwele Wilneuman, Grade 12

The Cheetah and the Donkey

Once upon a time in Namibia, there was a cheetah who would wander across the veld. Every day he would go to the kraal to eat a goat. He had to go through the donkey's pen. As you know, the cheetah is afraid of donkeys, so he would go through the pen when the donkey was asleep. But when the donkey heard the MAAAAAA! MAAAAAA! of the goat, he would awake and chase the cheetah. The very frightened cheetah would run as fast as he could to get away. He got used to it and he developed very long legs from running fast. Now he is the fastest animal on earth.

Amina Baird , Age 7

Grooming is an important part of a cheetah's life. Members of cheetah families spend many hours every day grooming each other with their rasp-like tongues. After meals they all help to clean each other's faces. Also, their very rough tongues help them to scrape the last bit of meat off bones.

The cheetah has long been confused with the leopard, the tiger and the panther, and the animal has been given different names in various languages. In the English expression, the cheetah was long known as the hunting leopard, and the Germans call it Gepard. In Dutch and Afrikaans the word for cheetah is jagluiperd. Chita, which is a Hindi word, came to be used in Africa by way of British colonial servants stationed in India, who hunted antelope with cheetahs.

1 the cheetah run fast

2 and He work glides

3 you can see He muscles

4 it aets meat

5 We people Extinct

6 the cheetah

7 the cheetah are all dying oat

8 We people must help the cheetahs

The Cheetah

Timid and shy
powerful and fast
hiding in the tallest grass

Tiny ears, amber eyes
in the sun the cheetah lies

When the cheetah
senses danger,
he prepares to fight the stranger

When the cheetah eats his prey
the lions and the leopards
often take it away

Then the cheetah has no food,
because the lion and the leopards
were so rude

So please understand the cheetah's plight,
for if you shoot him it won't be right

So don't let the cheetah become extinct,
it's the most beautiful animal on earth,
I think

Julie-Ann de Villiers, Age 14

Cheetahs usually hunt alone, and unlike leopards, they do not store their kills out of reach of other predators. This means they often have their hard-won meals stolen from them. Lions, hyenas, wild dogs and even vultures deprive them of their food.

The Catch

First light
On the open plain
A graceful curved-horn head
lifts...

Too late!
a burst of speed!
Lean, mean, running machine
Fluid strength and power
Reaching out, stretching forward
Muscles bunching, spots rippling,
ground covered in blur of motion
Flowing tail, streaming, graceful,
Balancing.
For one tangible second,
Claw extended,
Exploring...
Exploding in flesh!
Ripping, keenly gripping
Cat-like
Pouncing.
Long white canines sinking deeply
Taste of blood on hot tongue

Heat of hunt dissipating
in crisp cool morning air.
Purring
Satisfaction.

Pauline Scheeps, Adult

Cheetahs are "diurnal" hunters, which means they hunt in
the late morning and early evening. They capture their prey
by stalking it to within 10 - 30 meters before chasing it. The
cheetah trips the prey from the rear then grabs it by its
throat. The prey is suffocated when the cheetah bites the
underside of the throat. Chases typically last about 20
seconds and are rarely longer than one minute.
Approximately half of the chases are successful.

Jonas Murao, Grade 6

An Animal Built for Speed

Docile

The cheetah awakens
Adventure is dawning

A perfect piece of art
his body slender and sleek moves proudly
across the face of our land
Flowingly, gracefully
each step leaves his signature
a paw print embedded in the sands of Namibia

The sun pelts down from above
Just like the heart of the sun
the cheetah feels a blazing fire
a hunger

His movements transformed
cunning calculated steps of precision
The gun is cocked
Like a bullet, the cheetah is fired,
from a still statued stance
into the air
challenging the speed of light
Pounces
Pierces

Gnawing at the prey
Relishing the nourishment
Tearing
Devouring

This is an act of survival

Wendy Fernandez, Adult

*The natural prey of Namibia's cheetahs include kudu, oryx
and hartebeest calves, springbok, steenbock, other young
antelope, warthog, hare and game birds.*

George Tshaanika, Age 8

131

45

Die Jagluiperd

Stil rus'n slanke lyf op die klip.
Rustig lê hy daar en droom 'n Beweging indie
bosse laat hom wakker skrik. Sy gròen oë
glim, sy ore spits...

Versigtig beweeg die springbokke nader.
Hulle is sku.
Daar dreig gevaar...

Rats spring hy van die klip.
Koes-koes bekruip hysy prooi...

Stil lê die jagter agter sy geweer, elke spier in sy liggaam
styfgespan. 'n Beweging van die dier laat sy vinger
om die sneller krul. Die dier bespring sy prooi.
Die skoot knal!....sal die jagluiperd dit oorleef?

The Cheetah

The springbok drinks some nice cool water at the stream.
A beast of prey lies ten feet behind him under a bush.
He peers anxiously at the buck. He is very hungry.
His strong muscles get tense...
Suddenly, he jumps out of the bush!

Swiftly the buck runs away to find shelter, but it's too
late.
The cheetah gets him by the neck. The springbok kicks
and fights back bravely, but he slowly chokes.
Proudly the cheetah drags it under a bush and devours it.

Liezel Groenewald, Grade 5
Original in Afrikaans

*In the fifth century, cheetahs were used by Italian nobles to
hunt for sport, which was called "corusing." Cheetahs
were commonly known as "hunting leopards." Kublai
Khan, the founder of the Mongol dynasty in China, had
hundreds of cheetahs during the thirteenth century. Akbar, a
Mongolian ruler of the 16th century, was said to have
owned 9 000 cheetahs during his 49-year reign. Although
hundreds of cheetahs lived in captivity for hundreds of
years, they never bred in captivity until 1956.*

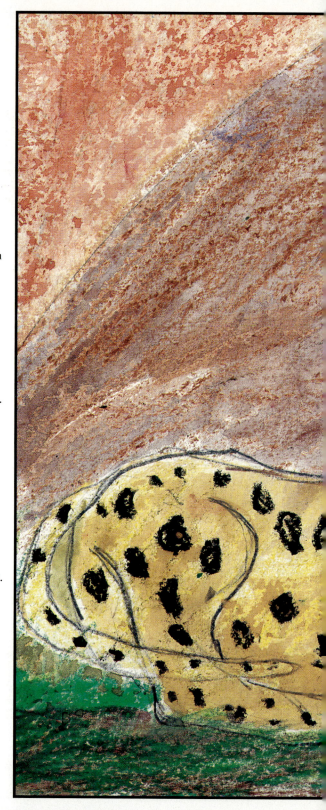

Matthew Marsh, Age 11

Cheetah
round
tears
Soft
Smooth
muscles
bristly

black
yellow

oval
kidney shaped

Stealthily

Susan Mujoro, Grade 1

The Cheetah

Beyond the dry and dusty plain
Longing thirstily for the rain
Two cheetah kittens, awaiting their mother,
Sleep comfortably one on top of the other.

Meanwhile Mum, tired and too trim
Desperately scans the horizon
The springbock have moved to better plains
Only rats and rabbits for hunger pangs.

The littlest kitten ventures out
To see what mother's all about
Weakly, hungrily, he's not aware
That danger – a puff adder – lingers near.

His tummy rumbling – he's far too thin
In dry time food's a battle to win;
He looks for Mum, clumsily too far,
One strike in his shoulder, it's all over now.

Just one kitten she finds, but purring and glad,
The lightning and thunder puzzle the lad;
Down pelt the drops! It's okay now Mum
Run happy and proud with your little son!

Gwen Currie, Grade 8

The average life expectancy of captive cheetahs is 8-12 years; longevity studies have not been conducted in the wild. However, researchers do know that cub mortality is high both in the wild and in captivity. On average, 20 percent of cubs born in captivity die within six months of birth. In Tanzania's Serengeti National Park, fewer than 5 percent survive to adulthood.

George Tshaanika, Grade 1

A Cheetah Named Dot

One little cheetah I named Dot,
he even had a mark like a spot.
He is all big and strong right now,
We used to feed him chopped-up cow.
When we run, he never comes last,
because he is very, very fast.
Some farmers want him to die,
but if they do I will cry.
All I know is he is strong,
and don't forget, very, very long.

Cuan-Jan Geyser, Grade 4

Male and female cheetahs are old enough to have offspring when they are one and a half to two years old. Their gestation, or period of pregnancy, is about 95 days or three months. The average litter size is four to five cubs, of which a very small number ever live to become adults. They are up to 30 centimetres long and weigh 250-300 grams at birth.

The Fate of Togo

It was a hot, sunny day. The McNeal's had a farm near the Okavango river called "Okavango Dream." Their four-year-old son, Michael, was playing in the cool shade on the front porch of the main house. His father was driving around on the farm fixing some fences while his mother was preparing lunch in their small but cozy kitchen.

No one saw little Michael leave. In time his mother realized that her son was gone. More than half an hour had passed. She and her farmworkers looked everywhere around the big house with no luck at all. In panic, she called Tom, her unsuspecting husband, over the walkie-talkie. Tom, afraid that something already could have happened to Michael, took the shortest way home. He asked Carol what exactly had happened and set out immediately to look for him.

As he was driving along the cheetah path, he saw a cheetah approaching something. He took his binoculars and was shocked! Through them, he saw his son's fair-haired head. He took his gun and shot. When he reached his son, he was astonished. Michael held the cheetah's cub in his lap.

At home they fed the little cheetah cub. His mother was very glad about Michael's return but very sad that her husband shot the cheetah's mother. Although it wasn't Tom's fault at all because he couldn't see the cub in Michael's lap, he felt tremendous guilt and decided that the cub should stay with them.

During the years Michael and Togo the cub became best friends. They grew up together and discovered the wonders of nature. Although Togo couldn't speak, his eyes and movements showed Michael how he was feeling. They grew so close that when Michael was eighteen and his fiancé came home with him from university, Togo was very jealous of her.

After they got married, Togo understood.
Michael's parents died shortly after their wedding. They didn't get to know their grandchild who was about to
be born.

One year later, after the arrival of Michael's son, Jason, Togo wasn't his old self anymore. He changed dramatically. He

Maike Lund, Age 13

became unaffectionate and unfriendly when he was with Jason, but it seemed to fade away after some time.

On Jason's second birthday, he went missing. Everybody went out looking for him. Only when more than half an hour had passed did Michael become aware of the fact that Togo was missing too! An indescribable feeling of fear crept into his heart. His son might be in danger! He was sweaty and nervous. Michael told everybody to stay home and he took his gun and went out to search. He kept searching until he saw Togo in the Cheetah path slowly approaching Jason. Michael's shaking hands took the gun, which once killed Togo's mother, aimed at Togo, took a long last look at him and pulled the trigger.

The next two days Michael lived in a state of trauma. He just went into the field, sat there and thought. He thought about how Togo and he grew up, what they did together and what they had learned fom each other. He would never forget the faithful look in Togo's eyes, his swift movements and his grace.

C. Bergendofer, Grade 12

Male cheetahs from the same litter live together in coalitions for their whole life, which increases hunting and mating success. When members of the coalition are live-trapped, relocated or killed, the remaining members may begin to hunt livestock because of their reduced numbers.

is a cheetah had round yas

is a cheetahcan run fast yas

a cheetah got spots

a cheetah legs is fast

cheetah skin is soft

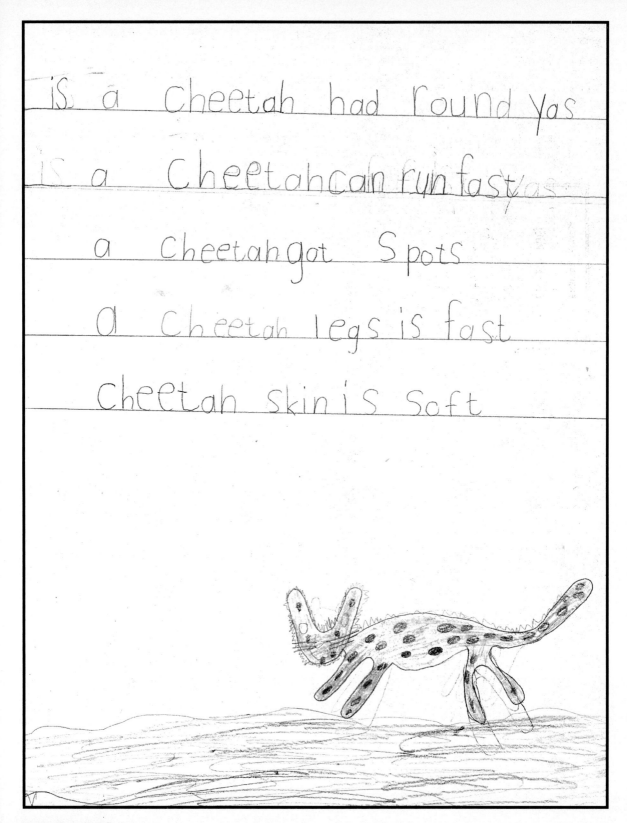

Danie Koen, Grade 1

"Saving" Suleika

It was the last day of the holidays and I was sitting in the sun, enjoying the last few hours before school started again. Everyone was tired from the day's work.

Suddenly something startled me. At first I did not know what it was, but then I saw the shepherd running towards me. He was gesticulating with his arms, jumping over the fence and stopping in front of me totally exhausted and shivering with fear. "What is wrong?", I asked. "There is a cheetah in the herd!" I told him to go to the car and wait, then I ran into the house and woke up my Dad. He, seeing the excitement in my eyes, jumped up while I was still explaining what was going on to him. He took the Winchester 308 and was on his way to the car.

While we were driving up the valley towards the herd, the shepherd told us what had happened. He said the cheetah virtually attacked him before he went into the herd. We were sure he only wanted to chase him away because he was between the cheetah and his prey. When we arrived we saw the cheetah's tracks and the Damara sheep that he had killed. The tracks were fascinating even though I had not seen the animal before. I knew I would be impressed by it. We drove back home to fetch the trap. We wanted to catch it in a trap that's like a big cage, where it has to walk in to get the prey.

An hour later we came back. The sheep were at home already and the prey was pulled under a tree. About one hundred metres away the cheetah was trotting – always looking back – into the mountains. The shepherd was sure that it was a leopard. But it was much too small for it, and one could see the clawmarks in the tracks.

At about four o'clock the trap was set and we went home again. My father wanted to check the trap before supper. When it was time we went out. It was dark already and when we approached the trap, we put on the spotlight. Suddenly two yellow spots were shining towards us. They looked so cold that I started to shiver. The eyes were moving a few steps to the left and back. He was in the trap! My father took the Winchester and went towards the cage, taking two men with him. It was only a hundred metres away, but it seemed like a long time before my father got there. I was still in the car holding the spotlight for them when he signalled to come with the car. Slowly I drove towards them and reversed the car to face the cage. I stopped the engine and walked to the back of the car.

I will never forget the first time I looked into those eyes. Eyes as big as a twenty-cent coin, pitch black and looking terrified. The tear stripes along the nostrils were highlighted by the color of the eyes. It was as if he looked at me in the hope of help. Not taking my eyes off the animal, I said as if in a trance, "Please don't

Magali Herbert, Age 12

kill him." No one said a word; only the breath of the cheetah broke the silence. After a while we decided to load him on the car with the cage and take him home. We did so, and unloaded him in the yard. He stayed there for the night.

My mother was moved deeply by the sight of her. She gave the cheetah - it was actually a female – the name, "Suleika." So it was decided that "Suleika" should live. But where?

The next morning we phoned the Cheetah Conservation Fund. They said they wanted Suleika, but it was too far for them to come and get Suleika. So they recommended we phone a man on a farm near the Hochveld. He was delighted to come and get her. That evening when everything for Suleika's new home was arranged, we left her on our farm and my Dad brought me to school.

After two weeks my Dad phoned me and told me that "Suleika" was on her way to her new "home." Nature Conservation was also there for the transfer. My Dad said that after two weeks of contact with him, hearing his voice, she had leaned against her cage and let my father scratch under her chin as she made purring sounds. So my Dad then decoyed her into the man's cage. Shortly afterwards they drove off.

This is a true story, and now I have this strange grip around my heart. I imagine "Suleika" in a cage of a few metres in size on that farm and I get a feeling of guilt. Her free life, her freedom, and, I'm sure, her vitality are now gone forever. She will forget how to hunt, how to survive in the wild. "Suleika" will never gain her strength back.

We saved her from death – but sent her to prison. Sometimes captivity is worse than death!

Nicole Theile, Grade 12

Cheetah cubs open their eyes at five to eleven days old. They begin to follow their mother when they are six weeks old, keeping very close to her and beginning to eat meat from the kills. The cubs remain with the mother until they are one-and-a-half years old, during which time she teaches them survival skills.

How The Cheetah Got His Spots

A long, long time ago when animals could still talk, there lived a cheetah. He was the only one from his species that survived. This cheetah had a beautiful gold skin and was very quick; therefore the other animals called him Blitz.

His prey could not easily escape him, and he could always find lots of wild animals, like rabbits, springbok, and hares. So, whenever he was hungry, he would go down to the river and he would always find something close by to eat.

One day Blitz was down by the river, getting ready to pounce on a springbok for lunch. But when he looked up, he saw a hunter's rifle pointed at him. Blitz became frightened and he ran and ran as fast as he could. Running was something that Blitz was very good at, so good in fact, that after a few minutes, he realized that he had run far away from home. Now he was in a strange place where nothing looked familiar and food was scarce and he was getting very hungry now.

Fortunately, Blitz came across a hare, and just as he was about to eat him, the hare begged him not to, promising Blitz that there were many hares nearby much fatter than he. Blitz grimaced suspiciously and told the hare to speak quickly if he wanted to live.

With that the hare walked over to a big, dangerous-looking rock and told the cheetah that he must strike the rock as hard as he could with two stones that the hare gave him. And so Blitz took the stones and hit the strange looking rock with all of his might. Well, it turned out that this big rock was actually a beehive and the next moment Blitz was being tackled by a swarm of bees. Blitz ran as quickly as he could to the nearest river and jumped into the water. Meanwhile, the hare ran in the other direction and managed to escape.

When Blitz got out of the water, he was covered in spots from all of the bee stings that he had received. The other animals asked him, "What happened to your beautiful gold skin?" He would just look angrily at them and walk by. In time though, he began to like his spots and he became proud of them because they made him look different from all of the other cats. But from that day forward, Blitz and the hare were bitter enemies.

Deon Jobs, Age 14

There are over 3 000 spots on an adult cheetah's coat.

Kaunawaye Philipus, Grade 10

A Miserable Life

I wasn't endangered all the time. There were plenty of my kind roaming the Great African Savannah – till Man came along. He killed all my friends just for their skins to be used as doormats and made into fur coats. He then chased us away from our land and put farms on it. Soon his cattle ate all of the grass. No grass was left for the wild antelopes. Soon my family began to starve. Our ribs began to show. We just had to eat, so one night we killed one of the farmer's animals. Soon he went around killing every cheetah in sight. He also killed my family in his wild rampage. Now I am left with no family, just some of my old pals. I live a cold and miserable life waiting to die. I need you to do something helpful. I don't want my kind to end up like the dodo bird – gone forever.

Fred Mule, Grade 7

extinct

The Cheetah

extinct the Feline Greyhound:
Hot arid extinctextinctextinctext
areas are his home. With it's inctex
small head and his small chest, tinct
long legs and flexible backbone extinct
it is known as a extinctextinctextinctex
swift tinctextinctextincte hunting feline .xt
inctextinctextinctextinct The cheetah is a
extinctextinct extinctex hunter of plains. He
tinctextinc reaches a speed tex
tinctexti of 110 km/h and
nctextinc is the fastest t
extinct of all land ext
inctex mammals .ti
nct extinctextincte
xtinctexHe hunts in
tinctexti the morning
and late afternoon
because then
heat is a prob-
lem for ctex
the tincte
cheet-xti
ah nct

I am a Cheetah in Namibia

Once upon a time there was a cheetah who was all alone. It lived near the mountains in the veld. It had no friends to play with. One day it decided to go and look for a friend. It walked and walked until it met a small bird which was singing. The bird stopped singing and asked "What do you want?" The cheetah answered, "I want to play with you." "What?" said the bird. "You want to play with me, but where are your wings?" The cheetah answered sadly, "I don't have wings." "So, go away," said the bird. The cheetah went away with a sad face.

Then it met a hare. The hare was jumping here and there. The cheetah came to the hare. "Good morning hare," said the cheetah.
"Good morning cheetah. What do you want?" asked the hare. "Oh!" said the cheetah "I want to play with you." "No, no you'll eat me," said the hare and ran away. So again the cheetah went away with a sad face.

The cheetah was hungry and decided to look for some fresh meat to eat. It met a lion who had caught a fat kudu. "Oh," roared the lion. "What do you want?" "I just want a piece of your meat," said the cheetah. "No, go away. It's not yours, so go!" The cheetah went away sadly.

It lay under a tree and started to cry. "No one wants to play with me," cried the cheetah. It cried for a long time until black tear marks appeared on its face. "Why are you crying?" asked the tortoise. "No one wants to play with me," said the cheetah. "Don't cry," said the tortoise. "Don't you know that you have a great talent?" said the tortoise. "You are the fastest animal in the world. You can run away from any problem if you want to," said the tortoise.

The cheetah was happy to hear this. It went away and never cried again. But the tear marks did not vanish.

Tuhandeleni Shikongo, Grade 6

The cheetah is the fastest mammal on earth. It can reach a top speed of 110 kilometres per hour in four seconds and can run 27 metres in one second. It can cover seven to eight meters in a single stride, with only one foot touching the ground at a time. At two points in the stride, none of its feet touches the ground. It can accelerate from zero to eighty kilometres in three seconds.

The Orphan Calf and the Magical Cheetah

Long ago there was a black man called Ntungi. He was 88 years old. Ntungi was a strong man, large, with black eyes, a hooked nose, big head, big teeth and bony feet. His skin was black and shining. He was a hard man and didn't like being with other people.

He lived in the Kavango near the river. It was very clean where he lived and there where many other people who lived with him in the same area. He built his house very well so that even if people tried to attack him during the night, they couldn't break in. He was fond of his house that was so expertly built.

He had lived in the Kavango for many years because he thought that there you could get everything. The most important thing was that there was enough grazing for his cattle. His cows, sheep and goats became fat and milkable. He got more milk in one week than most people get in one month. His sheep produced valuable wool that he could sell. He was a farmer and he always looked after his own cattle because he couldn't afford to employ someone else to do it.

One day, one of his cows was brutally killed by a hyena, so Ntungi set off with his gun into the forest to get his revenge and to bring the calf of the dead cow back to his farm to care for it. In the bush, while he was busy looking after his cattle, sheep and goats, he found to his surprise, a cheetah looking after a calf. He slowly realized that the calf in the care of this amazing cheetah was the very same calf whose mother had been killed by the hyena. Ntungi couldn't believe his eyes. He had never seen anything like it before.

The cheetah was the perfect parent. She protected the calf from lions and hyenas. She stopped the calf

64

Ewereth Muvangua, Age 15

from wandering too far and getting lost. In fact the calf had no intention of leaving her adopted mother.

But Ntungi took his calf back home. Many of his cows had a lot of milk, so he could feed the orphan calf. The orphan grew bigger and bigger. As the calf grew bigger and became an adult, it seemed that she too had magical powers. She could provide endless buckets of milk. Ntungi couldn't believe it.

Such was the power of this cow that Ntungi became a very rich man from selling all the milk. He was never sure, but he often thought that maybe the cow's strange up-bringing was the reason for its apparently magical powers. He never found or saw the cheetah again, though he often went to look for her in the hope of thanking her. But she had vanished like a magical wisp of smoke.

Augustinus Muronga, Age 20

Erna Hodës, Age 14

Cheetahs have been kept in captivity since 3 000 BC, when the Sumerians, in present-day Iraq, began taming them as pets. In Egypt, the pharaohs kept cheetahs as close companions as a symbol of protection from the goddess "Mafdet." Egyptians believed that the cheetah would carry the pharaoh's soul to the afterlife. The cheetah was admired for its speed, hunting ability and beauty, and it was honored as a symbol of royalty and prestige.

Der Ungkückliche Gepard

Der Gepard ist das schnellste Tier,
das wir in der Wildnis haben hier.
Hat er ein Zebra mal entdeckt,
hinterm Busch er sich versteckt.

Das Zebra, das entdeckt ihn nicht
es macht ein friedliches Gesicht.
Der Gepard denkt: "Das Tier ist dumm!
Doch gleich ist auch sein Leben um!"

Er springt, doch ruft dann; "Au! Oh nein!".
Er landet – *auf dem Stachelschwein!*
Das Zebra rennt, so schnell es kann,
in Richtung nächsten Wasserdamm.

Der Gepard sitzt am See der Toten,
zieht sich die Stacheln aus den Pfoten.
Doch plötzlich ruft er laut: "Oh weh!"
und fleigt kopfüber in den See!

Das Zebra steht am Ufer, lacht:
"Das habe ich fur dich gemacht!".
Das Zebra glücklich, ohne Frage:
Ein Gepard hat auch schwarze Tage.

The Unhappy Cheetah

The cheetah is the fastest animal
that we have in the wild here.
Once he found a zebra,
hiding behind a bush.

The zebra that saw him
makes a peaceful face.
The cheetah thinks, "This animal is stupid!
Soon also its life is gone!"

He jumps, but then cries, "Ugh! Oh no!"
He lands – *on a porcupine!*
The zebra runs, as fast as it can,
in the direction of the next dam.

continues

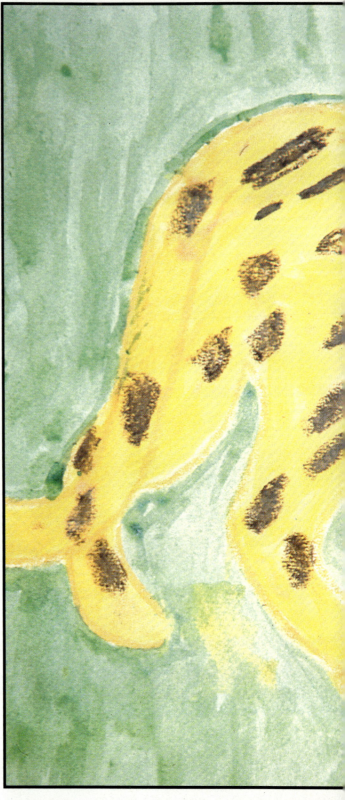

Edison Basson

WEARING US WON'T

DUPLICATE US !!

Sonja Kipping, Grade 10

The cheeetah sits at the Lake of the Death,
pulling out quills from his paws.
But suddenly he cries out loud: "Oh it hurts!"
and is flying in the lake head-first!

The zebra is standing at the shore, laughing:
"That is what I have done for you!"
The zebra was happy, without a doubt:
A cheetah also has bad days.

Benjamin Pfister, Age 9
Original in German

How The Cheetah Can Run So Fast

In the jungle, there lived a cheetah who aways dreamed of running fast. He was always late for everything. He was even slower then his friend, the tortoise. One day he decided to ask the King Lion to give him some strength so that he could run faster. He walked one kilometer for a whole week to get to the king's beautiful palace. Upon his arrival, the king was waiting for him. The animals had told him already that cheetah wanted to ask him something. The cheetah was too scared to talk, but then he asked the lion for strength to run faster. The lion said that he didn't have any strength to give him.

Many months passed and the cheetah was still sad. He wondered how he could get strength. One sunny day he found a dark forest when he went for a walk. He decided to explore this dark forest. He walked and walked for many days. The king of the jungle was worried because the animals didn't see him any more. Cheetah came to a big palace. He went inside and looked. He checked Room 118, and he saw a big bottle. Inside the bottle there was a small piece of chocolate. He went in and ate it. Suddenly he felt strange. He went outside. In a second, he was running so fast that his ears were hanging backwards. That is the how the cheetah became the fastest animal in the world. The cheetah lived happily ever after.

Peter-George Mannel, Grade 7

Glossary

Bottleneck – a severe population reduction, possibly resulting in the inbreeding of the remaining animals.

Carnivore – a meat-eating animal.

CITES – Convention on International Trade in Endangered Species of Wild Fauna and Flora. A treaty that monitors international trade in animals and plants. Over 115 countries have signed the Treaty. Namibia is a member nation, or "party," to CITES.

Conservation – the act of protecting and preserving the environment and wild species; and the wise use of natural resources.

Diurnal – active during the day and resting at night.

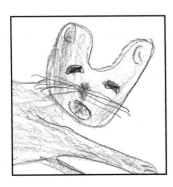

DNA – Deoxyribonucleic Acid. A chemical found in the chromosomes of every cell. DNA is organized into genes, which form the genetic code. An individual receives half of his or her DNA from the mother through her egg and half from the father's sperm.

Ecosystem – a biological community of plants, animals and other organisms together with the non-living components of their environments.

Endangered Species – a group of animals or plants in immediate danger of disappearing from the earth (becoming extinct) due to changes in their environment, loss of habitat, commercial trade and/or inability to adapt. Protective measures must be taken immediately or the species will become extinct. (The cheetah is an endangered species.)

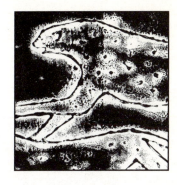

Environment – all the physical, chemical, and biological factors that affect or make up an organism's surroundings.

Extinct – no longer found on the earth, no longer living, gone forever.

Game Animal – legal designation for animals that may be hunted under regulation.

Gene – a unit of DNA responsible for determining a specific heritable trait (for example, brown hair). Mammalian DNA contains about 100 000 genes.

Genetic Diversity – the variety of genes in an organism or in a population.

Genus – a class, kind or group of animals or plants marked by common characteristics or by one common characteristic: a group capable of including subgroups and also being subsumed in a larger group.

Geographical Range – the area where an individual species of plant or animal population lives.

Habitat – the place where a species lives, the environment where a plant or animal naturally occurs.

Habitat Destruction – misuse and mismanagement an animal's natural habitat so that it can no longer survive there.

Holistic – the consideration of the ecosystem as a whole unit.

Home Range – the area where an animal roams during its normal activities.

Inbreeding – occurs when close relatives mate; after several generations of inbreeding, animals may exhibit poor reproductive traits, ill health, and short life-spans.

Litter – all the offspring of an animal produced at one birth.

Poaching – the illegal catching or killing of animals, or the illegal collecting of plants.

Population – the total number of individuals of a species that share the same geographic area.

Predator – an animal that hunts and kills other animals (**prey**) for its food.

Reserve – an area of land set aside to conserve and protect plants and animals.

Savannah – grassland with scattered trees.

Self-Sustaining Population – a population capable of maintaining or increasing its numbers without human intervention or assistance.

Semi-Retractable Claws – claws that can be only partially drawn back into their sheaths.

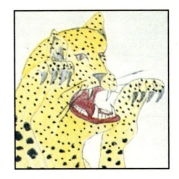

Species – a group of animals or plants of the same kind that breed and produce young like themselves. All organisms of the same kind.
(The leopard and cheetah are different species of cats.)

Sustainable Utilization – the wise use of wildlife and natural resources that allows the ecosystem to remain healthy.

Territory – the area of land in which an animal lives and defends as its home. Animals may have fierce fights over territorial land.

Wildlife – non-domesticated animals.

Wildlife Management – overseeing and utilizing an ecosystem to ensure its survival.

Much of the glossary information has come from the CCF's Teacher's Resource Guide, *Cheetahs: A Predator's Role in the Ecosystem.*

Cheetah Conservation Fund

The Cheetah Conservation Fund (CCF), a registered Namibian Trust, was founded by Laurie Marker-Kraus and Daniel Kraus in 1990 to secure the survival of cheetahs and their ecosystems. It is the first international organization created to support conservation research programs for the free-ranging cheetah. CCF conducts independent and collaborative research, disseminates information and recommends conservation management techniques. The multi-faceted holistic approach undertaken by CCF includes: (1) an extensive public education and awareness campaign; (2) a conservation research program; and (3) livestock and wildlife management plans.

Since 1991, CCF has conducted an aggressive conservation and environmental education campaign to ensure inclusion of the cheetah, *Acinonyx jubatus*, an endangered species worldwide, in environmental education programs for Namibian school children, as well as for the general public.

Long-term conservation research of the cheetah throughout its range is an integral part of CCF's program. CCF's research focuses on three areas of discovery. First, is the identification of important components of farmland ecosystems necessary to sustain healthy cheetah populations. Second, is the collection of biological samples to aid in the development of an extensive database on wild cheetah populations. Third, is the radio-tracking of cheetahs to learn more about their movements through farms and to monitor cheetahs in areas where new livestock and wildlife management practices are being tested.

To survive, the cheetah must have a habitat and a prey base. These essential elements can be maintained through a holistic approach on the farmlands that incorporates land use, livestock and wildlife. CCF believes the goal should be to balance the needs of the people with those of the cheetah.